Remember This

By Jenny Oates Riggs

Illustrated by Dennis Auth

BELLE ISLE BOOKS
www.belleislebooks.com

ISBN 978-1-947860-01-8

LCCN 2017960585

Printed in the United States

Published by

Belle Isle Books

BELLE ISLE BOOKS

www.belleislebooks.com

Dedication

To my mom, Gloria Jackson Oates,
whose beautiful legacy has given me much to remember.

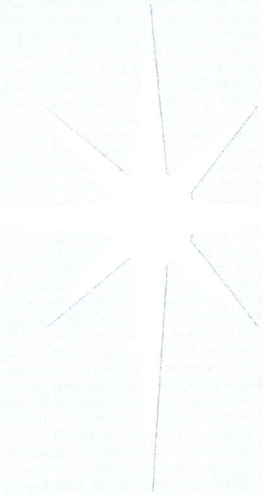

You'll gaze at Dad on a cold night
as he handpicks the best tree…
but remember the perfect tree created in the garden.

You'll lend a hand to decorate the tree,
adding treasured ornaments and a star to the top…
but remember the star that led the wise men from afar.

You'll enjoy building a gingerbread town out of sweets…
but remember the town of Bethlehem where
Joseph and Mary's journey took them.

You'll watch Mom busily wrapping presents…
but remember the baby wrapped in swaddling clothes.

You'll stride alongside Auntie
as she shops in each and every store for gifts….
but remember the most important gift is God's son, Jesus!

You'll hear the sweet sound of Mom
joyfully humming carols throughout the house…
but remember the angels who greeted the shepherds
and joyfully praised His name!

You'll feel the uncomfortable scratchiness
of your fancy shirt as you head to church…
but remember how Jesus had to be
in His Father's house.

You'll find your baby sister
enjoying a festive candlelit cleansing…
but remember, the most powerful cleansing offered
is the forgiveness of sin.

You'll be tempted to shake
and guess what treasures lay under the tree…
but remember the One who was greatly tempted.

You'll delight in hearing neighbors caroling
"The Twelve Days of Christmas" to spread cheer…
but remember the twelve disciples
chosen to spread His good news.

You'll peacefully sleep
while visions of sugarplums
dance in your head...
but remember while Jesus slept,
waves danced against the boat's side,
until He said, "Be still!"

You'll pass long lines of giddy children,
desperate to sit on Santa's knee…
but remember that Jesus welcomed
all the little children to Him.

You'll finally get to visit that man
sitting high in a chair, dressed all in red…
but remember, the Man who now sits on a throne
was once covered in red.

You'll sit down to watch
one of your family's favorite classic movies…
but remember when Jesus asked 5,000 people
to sit down and took care of their needs.

You'll warmly snuggle into bed
to listen to Dad read a wintertime story…
but remember how the people listened
to Jesus as He told stories.

You'll attend a parade with enthusiasm,
surrounded by the excitement of a waving crowd…
but remember the jubilant crowd
that waved palm branches as He entered Jerusalem.

You'll spy your big brother going into his room
and closing the door to wrap presents in secret…
but remember how Jesus taught us
to go into a quiet place to pray.

You'll watch your sister
lacing her feet up tightly in skates…
but remember how Jesus washed the feet of his disciples.

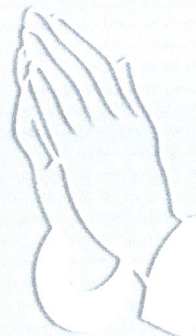

You'll taste all the scrumptious family favorites
at Christmas supper…
but remember the Last Supper,
when Jesus told of the cross to come.

You'll create a colorful paper chain
to count down to the eventful day…
but remember the chains that led Him
to the day it was finished.

You'll tear through shiny packages
until each one is empty…
but remember the empty tomb
that once held His body.

You'll help tack mistletoe
onto doorframes until each branch is hung…
but remember how His body hung for us.

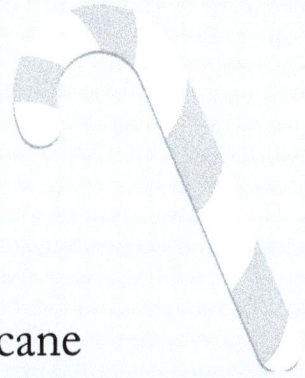

You'll savor every lick of a candy cane
with its sweet mix of red and white mint…
but remember that Jesus shed
His red blood to make our sins white as snow.

You'll hear the joyous sounds
of family and friends who visit…
but remember the joy that Jesus' friends shared
when they knew He was alive!

You'll listen to Mom's instructions
as you wait for the fun to begin…
but remember the most important instructions given -
Believe and Tell others!

You'll start a battle by beaning your brother
in the back with a large snowball…
but remember, a battle was waged
and the enemy has been defeated.

You'll feel a tug at your heartstrings
as decorations are boxed up,
knowing you'll have to wait for their return…
but remember there is One greater
whose return we're enthusiastically waiting for!

You'll witness Grandma
sharing her freshly baked cookies…
but remember to be a witness,
and share the good news with others.

You'll read about a little green fellow
whose heart grows bigger…
but remember, your heart holds the Spirit
and the power He possesscs.

You'll view lights in each frosted window…
but remember that Christ is the light of the world.

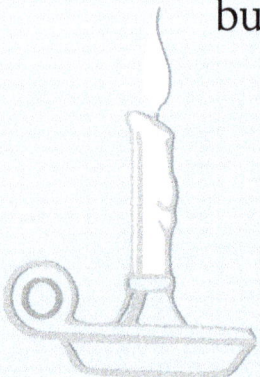

About the Author

Jenny Riggs' dad told her, "Dream big," and Jenny took it to heart. First, she earned a master's degree in teaching. Then, at an obstetrician's appointment, she heard a heartbeat and realized her second dream was to be a stay-at-home mom. Now, many years and three kids later, she's hardly ever home. Among sports practices, grocery store stops, and playground visits, she finds joy in her daughter's imagination, her son's dimples, braiding her youngest's hair, and having date nights with her man. On the weekend, Jenny likes to paint old furniture, tour museums, and worship at church. She kills every plant she touches, enjoys french fries a little too much, and visits coffeehouses for the hot chocolate. It was in a coffeehouse, sipping cocoa, that another dream came to light as she penned *Remember This*.

About the Illustrator

Dennis Auth hails from Pittsburgh, Pennsylvania, where teaching guitar and leading a band landed him in art school, inspiring instructors and fellow design students alike. He began freelancing after relocating as an ad-agency art director to Virginia Beach, where he illustrated in multiple media for projects ranging from children's books to striking architecture. The Tidewater area is home to Dennis, his wife, and their grown children.

www.ingramcontent.com/pod-product-compliance
Lightning Source LLC
Chambersburg PA
CBHW060944100426
42813CB00016B/2858